— PE⬤PLE T⬤ KN⬤W —

WALT DISNEY
Creator of Mickey Mouse

Michael D. Cole

ENSLOW PUBLISHERS, INC.

44 Fadem Road	P.O. Box 38
Box 699	Aldershot
Springfield, N.J. 07081	Hants GU12 6BP
U.S.A.	U.K.

Library of Congress Cataloging-in-Publication Data

Cole, Michael D.
    Walt Disney : creator of Mickey Mouse / Michael D. Cole.
       p. cm. —(People to know)
    Includes bibliographical references and index.
    Summary: Relates the life of the master of animation and founder of
Disneyland including both personal and professional endeavors.
    ISBN 0-89490-694-1
    1. Disney, Walt, 1901–1966—Juvenile literature. 2. Animators—United
States—Biography—Juvenile literature. [1. Disney, Walt, 1901–1966. 2. Motion
pictures—Biography.] I. Title. II. Series.
NC1766.U52D532 1996
791.43'092—dc20
    [B]   95-31202
                                                CIP
                                                AC

Printed in the United States of America

10 9 8 7 6 5 4 3 2 1

Illustration Credits: UPI/Bettmann, pp. 4, 11, 31, 34, 47, 49, 58, 63, 72,
76, 79, 83, 85, 95, 98, 101

Cover Illustration: UPI/Bettmann

Contents

Walt Disney

1

Disney, Disney Everywhere

Walt Disney wore a broad smile as he stooped to greet the young girl and boy who had just passed through the gate as the first visitors to Disneyland. The date was July 17, 1955, and the Anaheim, California, sun was shining brightly on Disneyland's opening day.

Shortly after those first two children, thousands of other visitors poured through the gate that day. They came to enjoy the rides and exhibits as well as all the sights and sounds of the incredible new amusement park. The cement was still soft in some places, there were complaints about too few drinking fountains, and some of the rides broke down. But after a few days the park was running like a well-oiled machine.

As Walt Disney strolled the grounds in the following days and weeks looking for ways to further improve the park, he was very pleased to see that the park's visitors—young and old—were having a wonderful time. A mere seven weeks later, the one millionth visitor passed through the entrance of Disneyland.

Walking down the streets of Disneyland, a visitor was sure to see some colorful characters. These imaginative figures all shared one trait in common—they were all the brainchild of Walt Disney.

Children screamed with delight at the sight of Donald Duck, Goofy, and Pluto. Adults smiled as children shook hands and exchanged hugs with Snow White and the Seven Dwarfs, and Pinocchio and Jiminy Cricket.

Then, of course, there was Mickey Mouse. Mickey had started it all for Walt Disney. In 1928 Mickey Mouse starred in *Steamboat Willie*, the first sound cartoon. Walt Disney provided not only the voice for Mickey Mouse, but his engaging and universally appealing personality. Twenty-seven years later, when Disneyland opened in 1955, Mickey Mouse was still the most popular cartoon character in the world.

The Mickey Mouse Club television show debuted in October of that same year. Before long, children all over America were singing the show's familiar theme: "Who's the leader of the club that's made for you and me? M-I-C-K-E-Y M-O-U-S-E."[1]

Success continued to follow Disney. Early in 1955 Disney's spectacular film version of *20,000 Leagues*

Under the Sea proved a sensation at theaters. In the summer the latest Disney animated feature, *Lady and the Tramp*, was yet another big hit.

The second season of the *Disneyland* television show kicked off with the movie *Dumbo*. The *Disneyland* program had already helped promote the opening of the Disneyland theme park. Now *Disneyland* was the most popular show on television. It was popular because it did what all Disney creations did—stimulate the imaginations of people of all ages.

Even after his death, Walt Disney is still stimulating the imaginations of millions the world over. His creative visions are still with us. This is because their power was matched only by his ambition to see those visions become reality. In the thirty-eight years that he lived after the first appearance of Mickey Mouse, Disney heavily influenced the motion picture and entertainment industry. He greatly changed the face of American popular culture.

The influence of Walt Disney is, in fact, almost inescapable. The images of his characters are all around us—on everything from videocassettes to T-shirts, from bedsheets to bottles of bubble bath.

But who was Walt Disney? This is not an easy question to answer. He was a man who by the end of his life was already a legend. He was very rich and famous, although he never sought wealth or fame. He enjoyed

them, of course, but to Walt Disney, money and reputation were usually just a means to an end.

What drove Walt Disney, day in and day out, was the desire to create. He was a man who found his happiness and fulfillment in creating things that he thought would entertain and make other people happy. And over the years, his visions grew bigger and bigger.

Walt Disney's vision and ambition were driven by a zestful creativity that made him one of the most unique men of the twentieth century. He grew up in America's heartland as that century was just beginning.

2

Farm Boy, Newsboy, Train Boy

"Pa always had ants in his pants," said Walt Disney's brother Roy about their father Elias Disney. "He could never stay in one place long enough to warm a seat."[1]

Elias Disney had already lived in Kansas, Colorado, and Missouri before any of his children were born. He had worked as a carpenter on the railroad line and as a mail carrier. He had bought and sold an orange grove in Florida, and had even panned—unsuccessfully—for gold in California.

While in Florida, Elias married a young woman named Flora Call on New Year's Day, 1888. Later the couple had their first son, Herbert. After selling the orange grove, Elias moved the family to Chicago, Illinois. There, he went into business as a carpenter and home builder in the expanding midwestern city. With a steady income, Elias had little trouble supporting a growing family, which soon included sons Raymond and Roy.

Flora was pregnant again in 1901, and so was the wife of the family's preacher, Walter Parr. "If I get a boy baby, I'll name him after you," Elias told Parr. "And if your baby is a boy, you name him after me." The preacher agreed. Flora Disney had a baby boy on December 5, 1901. Elias kept his word to Walter Parr by naming his fourth son Walter Elias Disney.[2]

Two years later, in 1903, Flora gave birth to their only daughter, Ruth Flora Disney. In the years just after Ruth's birth, Elias began to notice the changing nature of the city around him. The close family ties that once made up the community were breaking down, and crime was becoming a serious problem.

Two local boys the same age as Elias's oldest sons were sentenced to prison for killing a police officer during a robbery. That was when Elias decided it was once again time to move. After visiting his brother in Marceline, Missouri, Elias decided that town's rural atmosphere was the place that he wanted to finish raising his family.

The Disneys arrived in Marceline in 1906. Elias bought a forty-five-acre farm not far from town. Here, Walt Disney spent his formative childhood years. Walt had no memory of his early years in Chicago, so the farm

Walt Disney's parents, Flora and Elias Disney, as they appeared
in 1938.

in Marceline became the scene of his earliest memories as well as the birthplace of his imagination.

Walt's older brothers—Herbert, Raymond, and Roy—were all in their teens by then. Elias worked them very hard on the farm, growing corn, wheat, sorghum, and barley as well as raising cows, pigs, and chickens to feed the family. Walt and his younger sister were not old enough or strong enough to take on the same responsibilities. Walt mostly helped with his mother's chores. That is, when he was not playing in the barns or running around with his special pet pig he had named Porker.

Walt had an admirer and constant tagalong in his little sister Ruth. She was with Walt for one of his first artistic experiments—an ill-advised painting with tar. Their parents had gone into town, leaving Walt, aged seven, and Ruth, aged five, to entertain themselves on the farm. It was not long before Walt discovered a big barrel of tar and started playing with it. Walt, who was very sure of himself, confidently explained to Ruth that the tar could be used just like paint. To demonstrate, he dipped a stick in the bucket of black sticky tar and began painting on the side of his parents' white house.

After Walt had painted a few pictures of houses with smoke rising from their chimneys, Ruth began to wonder if Walt's idea was wise.

"Will this come off?" she asked.

"Oh, sure," Walt replied as he painted.[3]

Walt seemed so sure about the tar that Ruth picked up a stick of her own and started painting zigzags under Walt's houses. After a while they stopped to admire their work. Only then did Walt discover the first houses he had painted were now dry and hardened on the wall. They would not come off!

When Elias came home and saw the drawings, he immediately gave Walt a whipping with a long, thin apple tree branch. But the sting from the whipping wore off long before the drawings on the house. The tar drawings were a constant reminder of Walt's mistake, for they stayed on the house as long as the Disneys lived on the Marceline farm.

In another bout of creativity, Walt discovered a pile of old burlap bags and decided to sew them together into a tent. With a tent and a couple of the family cats, Walt decided he would put on a circus. He charged a handful of friends and neighbors ten cents to see the little show in the burlap tent. However, circus master Walt had made a mistake in his choice of animals to train. He discovered too late that cats are unpredictable performers. The show was a flop, and Walt's mother made him give back the profits.

Unfortunately for historians, Walt Disney's earliest drawings were not preserved. Since paper was scarce on the farm, Walt resorted to drawing on toilet paper. For obvious reasons, those drawings did not survive. Most of what Walt drew on those sheets of toilet paper were pictures of the farm animals that surrounded him. He was very fond of the animals, especially the pigs and chickens. One chicken named Martha would come and lay an egg in his hand when he called her by name.

His favorite animal was a pig named Porker. Walt later said:

> I guess I really loved that pig. . . . She had an acute sense of fun and mischief. . . . Do you remember the Foolish Pig in *Three Little Pigs?* Porker was the model for him.[4]

Relatives often visited the Disney's Marceline farm, and Walt's favorite relative was his Uncle Ed Disney. Ed was essentially a hobo who traveled the countryside working odd jobs for food and whatever money he needed to get himself from place to place.

Walt liked his Uncle Ed because he brought candy and chewing gum—sweets Elias forbid his children to have. Walt would secretly chew the gum, then stick it under the porch railing where he could retrieve it for chewing the next day. Ed also shared Walt's love of animals. Walt was always amazed at how Ed could get wild birds to sit on his shoulder and field mice to eat cheese from his hand or nestle in his pockets.[5]

Walt started school in Marceline when he was almost seven. He was a well-behaved student, but a problem for his teachers when it came to learning. His degree of self-confidence at an early age made it difficult for teachers to convince him of the importance of learning arithmetic. While they stood at the chalkboard teaching the class, Walt sat at his desk doodling. At some point during his two years at the Park School in Marceline, Walt carved his initials in his desk.

During these years, Walt developed a closeness with his brother Roy. Although he was eight years older than Walt, Roy was a kind and sensitive young man who liked to help his younger brother, often encouraging his natural creativity. Roy simply seemed to enjoy making Walt happy. When Roy earned some extra money working for a neighboring farmer, instead of spending it on himself, he would buy Walt a toy or a set of paper and sketch pencils.

From these very early days, the relationship between Roy and Walt took shape. It would follow the same pattern for the next sixty years. At first Roy only nurtured Walt's vivid imagination and boundless creativity. But eventually Roy would find himself raising money and overcoming real-world obstacles to bring Walt's imaginary worlds to life.

The Disney family hit hard times when Walt's other two brothers, Herbert and Raymond, left home. When Herbert was nineteen and Raymond seventeen, the two boys left a note one night saying that they had run away to Kansas City to make a life of their own.

A short time after the oldest boys left, the Disney's pigs were stricken with swine fever. Then a few days later Elias was diagnosed with a bad case of typhoid, a serious disease caused by bacterial infection. The source of the disease was the farm's well water, which was now deemed unsuitable for drinking. The contaminated well water and the departure of the oldest sons made it impossible for the Disneys to continue living and working on the farm. While Elias recovered from typhoid during the harsh winter of 1908–1909, Roy and Walt had a job to do. They walked through the heavy snows posting signs in the local area to announce the upcoming auction of their farm.

The family did well at the auction. The farm fetched a good enough price to pay off all debts and still leave enough money to move to Kansas City. Soon after arriving in the city, Elias obtained a franchise from the circulation departments of the local newspapers— the *Times*, the *Evening*, and the *Sunday Star*. The department heads were uncertain about entrusting the delivery of so many newspapers to fifty-year-old Elias, who was looking old and frail after his illness. But Elias's plan amounted to this—he would get the delivery franchises and the money, while Roy and Walt would deliver the newspapers.

Delivering the papers on frigidly cold icy mornings was terribly hard work for the ten-year-old Walt. He would make his rounds in the morning, go to school until the afternoon, return to the newspaper office after school, and then make the rounds again with the evening newspaper. There was no rest on Sundays, which were almost the worst days. Walt had to struggle to deliver the Sunday paper that was awkwardly bulging with advertisements.

Elias soon expanded his delivery areas and hired additional newsboys to make those deliveries. He paid those newsboys, but Roy and Walt never saw a dime. This unacceptable arrangement drove the seventeen-year-old Roy, like his two older brothers, to leave home. He soon took a job as a clerk at a Kansas City bank.

Walt's brother Herbert arrived back on the family scene at about the same time that Elias was feeling the itch to move again. Herbert had been working in the city since leaving the Marceline farm. Now Elias wanted to sell the delivery franchises to Herbert. Then he could move himself and the family back to Chicago, where a friend had a job for him in a jelly factory. This friend wanted Elias to assist in managing the jelly factory, which was soon to expand into soft drink production. Elias strongly believed that this was his opportunity to get rich, so he made the move. But Flora insisted that she stay behind in Kansas City with Ruth and Walt until they were finished with their terms in school.

This arrangement suited Walt fine. Unknown to his father, Walt had secretly bought a small newspaper route of his own. He had been earning some spending money while delivering his father's papers. He kept the route, sold it when school let out, then lied about his age to take a job as a "news butcher." He worked selling newspapers, candy, soda pop, cigarettes, and matches on the Pacific Railroad that ran between Kansas City and Jefferson, Missouri. That wonderful summer of 1917 was one of the favorite times of Walt's life. He had his first taste of independence and developed a lifelong love of trains.[6]

"What more could a young boy want?" Disney later asked. "I was seeing the world and earning money while doing it! In addition, I didn't have my father always hovering over me, badgering me."

The straight-laced, no-nonsense Elias Disney scoffed at Walt's ambitions to become an artist. "I don't want anyone to think my father was a tyrant, but he did have a terrible temper, and he was always trying to make you do things for which you weren't suitable."[7]

Walt finally followed his family to Chicago and entered McKinley High School in the fall of 1917. Some of his drawings were printed in the school newspaper, but the quality of the drawings was crude and the jokes accompanying them poor. In an effort to improve his talent, he enrolled in night classes at the Chicago Academy of Fine Arts. While attending these classes three nights a week, he met cartoonists from the Chicago newspapers. One of them, Leroy Gossett of the *Chicago Tribune*, showed Walt around the *Tribune* office and introduced him to his co-workers.

After the visit to the newspaper staff office, Walt

knew what he wanted to do. He now saw a job where he could draw and make good money at it. He wanted to become a newspaper cartoonist.[8]

But something else was happening that would, temporarily at least, set aside the personal ambitions of many young American men at that time. That rather significant event was called World War I.

3

The Young Cartoonist

In 1917 the United States entered World War I, and Walt's brothers Roy and Raymond immediately enlisted in the Navy. After Walt visited Roy during his training at the Great Lakes Naval Station outside of Chicago, Walt was ready to enlist as well. He had just graduated from high school and was hooked on the romanticism of going off to war in Europe. But his road to the war was full of obstacles.[1]

At age sixteen, he was too young to enlist without his parents' consent. Elias and Flora had no intention of letting Walt be their third son, after Roy and Raymond, to go off to war. But Walt was determined. He told his parents, "I don't want my grandchildren asking me, 'Why weren't you in the war? Were you a slacker?'"[2]

Walt once again lied about his age, and forged his

parents' name on a passport so that he could go over to France as part of the Red Cross Ambulance Corps.[3] However, he was not sent to France until after the armistice was signed, ending the war in November 1918. In December, Walt was one of fifty men from the South Beach, Connecticut, Red Cross Station who were sent to France to care for the sick and wounded American soldiers still overseas.

Upon his arrival, he found himself in demand as a driver. He not only drove a Red Cross ambulance, but he chauffeured officers and other high-ranking military officials all over France and the occupied part of Germany. In his spare time he wrote illustrated letters home to his family and friends in Chicago. He also painted caricatures of his fellow volunteers on the canvas sides of the Red Cross Jeeps.

Before returning home, Walt and a friend hatched a scheme to make some extra money. They bought surplus German helmets and shot bullet holes through them. Then Walt painted German military insignia or camouflage over the helmets to make it appear as though they had been used in actual combat. Walt and his friend sold these "genuine" German combat helmets as souvenirs to American soldiers returning home. The little scam earned Walt nearly $300—more money than he had ever seen in his life!

He was not yet eighteen years old when he returned by steamship to New York in the fall of 1919. In New

York he took in the tall buildings and visited motion picture houses to see two new Charlie Chaplin comedies. Soon he headed home to Chicago. Elias Disney told him that he could work with him in the jelly factory for $25 a week, but Walt told him that he was not interested.

When Elias asked Walt what he wanted to do, Walt replied that he wanted to become an artist. Elias next asked him how he expected to make a living as an artist. Walt admitted that he did not know.[4]

He soon packed up his suitcase and left Chicago for Kansas City, where his brother Roy had returned after the war to take a job as a bank teller. Walt tried to get work as a cartoonist with the Kansas City newspapers, but had no success. He reported his troubles to Roy. His brother had a friend at the bank who knew two commercial artists seeking an apprentice. Roy immediately told Walt to apply at the Pesmen-Rubin Commercial Art Studio in the Gray Advertising Building. Walt met the two artists, who were impressed by his artwork and attitude. Walt was thrilled when they told him to report for work the next day.[5] It was his first real job as an artist.

Disney made drawings for advertisements and letterheads. Most of his work was for farm equipment companies and other agriculture-related firms. His drawings included hens laying eggs and cows licking salt blocks. Pesmen-Rubin also did department store advertising and had the account for the local Newman

Theater. Disney drew the artwork for the covers of the theater's programs as well as the illustrations for its newspaper advertisements. The theater artwork gave him a little more room to exercise his creativity.

Another eighteen-year-old working at Pesmen-Rubin was a fellow named Ub Iwerks. Iwerks did lettering and airbrush work for the agency, and had been hired a month before Walt arrived. However, after the December holiday rush of department store and theater advertising, both Disney and Iwerks were let go from the agency.

The two young artists were now out of work. Although they had received their first few paychecks as artists at Pesmen-Rubin, they now had few options in the city to continue working as artists. Because they knew that work would be very hard to find, Disney and Iwerks seriously discussed going into business for themselves. Even if they could find work, the two young men reasoned, they could make more money in business for themselves than they could working for another agency.

Disney wrote to his mother and told her to send the $500 he had made with the Red Cross, explaining that he needed it to start a business. The new company was to be called "Disney-Iwerks," but after seeing their listing in the lobby of the Railroad Exchange Building, the partners decided it sounded too much like an eyeglass company. They changed the name to Iwerks-Disney

Commercial Artists, and Disney and Iwerks began their first days as business partners.

Their first assignment was artwork for the journal of the United Leatherworkers' Union. Iwerks-Disney earned $135 the first month—more money than the two had made working for Pesmen-Rubin. Unfortunately, few other contracts came their way.

Then, in January 1920, Iwerks saw an ad in the newspaper for a cartoonist. Although their business together had just barely gotten started, the unselfish Iwerks felt Disney should try for the job. Disney interviewed for the position and was hired. He stayed in touch with Iwerks while beginning work with the Kansas City Film Ad Company. Disney made drawings for a crude form of animated cartoons used as commercials in theaters.

Animated cartoons were just developing by 1920. In 1919 Felix the Cat had become the first highly popular cartoon character. The character was created by Pat Sullivan and Otto Messmer. Felix's success was due to the fact that its creators had blended the physical comedy styles of silent movie comedians Charlie Chaplin and Buster Keaton into their own animated character. The successful work of other animators in New York—such as Winsor McKay, and Max and Dave Fleischer—were adding to the popularity of animated cartoons.

Kansas City Film Ad's one-minute cartoon

commercials were hits with local theater-goers simply because they were animated. Their popularity brought about the demand for more cartoonists, and Disney strongly recommended that the company hire Ub Iwerks. Disney and Iwerks were working together again, but Disney already had his eyes set on something more satisfying—something more creative.

Disney did the drawings for his cartoons, but he did not do the camerawork or any other steps in developing the animation. He observed and studied all steps in the animation process and checked out books on animation from the library. As would become his trademark, Disney began looking for ways to improve both the technology and the artistic quality of the animation process.

After days of begging one of the company's owners to let him borrow a camera, Disney began experimenting with it in a makeshift cartoon studio in his garage. He was up past midnight every night, experimenting with different kinds of drawings, trying new camera angles, and adjusting the angle and intensity of the lighting. During these late-night sessions, he forged his new-found techniques into his own cartoons—all with a local twist that would have an interest to local theater patrons. After completing a set of cartoons, he sold them to the Newman Theater under the title of "Newman Laugh-O-Grams."[6]

Walt Disney was now a very busy young man. He

worked at Kansas City Film Ad during the day and on his Newman Laugh-O-Grams at night. In the midst of all his work, his situation at home greatly changed.

The jelly factory in which Elias Disney had invested all his money collapsed. Soon after, Walt's father, mother, and sister Ruth returned to Kansas City to live in the house Walt was sharing with his brothers Roy and Herbert, and Herbert's wife. So for a time the small house held seven people. But by the fall of 1921 the house was empty.

Herbert Disney was transferred to a job in Portland, Oregon. Soon after Herbert's departure, Roy was diagnosed with tuberculosis and sent for treatment to a veterans' hospital in California. Tuberculosis, very common during those years, is a chronic disease of the lungs. At the time the disease often lasted for years, and Roy Disney's chances of recovery did not look good. Then Elias and Flora took Ruth with them to Oregon, where Herbert and his wife had just had their first child.

With his family gone from Kansas City, Walt Disney was alone and he devoted himself entirely to his work. He took a small apartment for himself. Then he found some young artists interested in cartooning who agreed, for no pay, to help him with his Laugh-O-Gram cartoons. Disney had a talent for making people, both young and old, believe in the future success and profits of his ventures. The twenty-year-old cartoonist-entrepreneur soon convinced a number of Kansas City professionals to invest $15,000 in his Laugh-O-Gram cartoon projects.

The first project, *Little Red Riding Hood*, looked good, so Walt incorporated Laugh-O-Gram Films in early 1922. He immediately convinced Ub Iwerks to quit his job at Kansas City Film Ad and join him. He also hired five other animators in their late teens. With long hours and little pay, Disney and his young animators produced short cartoons of *Jack and the Beanstalk*, *Cinderella*, and other fairy tales.

Disney's staff soon grew to ten animators. He did some animation, some camerawork, and even washed the animation celluloids so that they could be used again. Celluloids, called "cels," were the transparent sheets on which the animation was inked. Disney also kept the company financially afloat by using the camera to film news events for a New York newsreel company. In addition, he took baby pictures for local parents. The work was long and hard.

Still, the earnings were not enough. His poorly paid animators were leaving, and it looked as though Laugh-O-Gram Films was going to fail. Then Disney had a new idea—combining his cartoon animation with photography of a live-action child actress. Using this technique Walt and his animators began creating a short film called *Alice's Wonderland*. The film looked promising, and Disney managed to find a film distributor in New York who could distribute his cartoons in theaters throughout the country.

Unfortunately, in the middle of production, Disney completely ran out of money. When he called Roy in California to describe his troubles, Roy told him, "Kid, I think you should get out of there."[7]

Disney's company declared bankruptcy in the spring of 1923. The owner of the failed cartooning company was only twenty-one years old. The company's failure had been a tough blow for Disney, and he wanted to put the experience behind him. He wanted to make a fresh start for himself by moving to either New York or California. Roy told him to come out West.

Disney paid off his debts and raised money for his train ticket by shooting more film for a New York newsreel company. The young Disney still had his pride. He worked until he could afford a first-class ticket to California. With everything he owned in one large suitcase, Walt hopped on the train. He was headed for Hollywood.

4

The Hard Bumps
of Hollywood

At twenty-one, Walt Disney had already produced and
directed several of his own cartoons. He hoped that his
experience might qualify him to be a movie director in
Hollywood. Disney arrived in Hollywood during the
wild days of silent movie production. Gloria Swanson
and Rudolph Valentino were the great stars drawing
crowds to the theaters. The large studios—such as
MGM, Warner Bros., and Paramount—had not yet
taken hold in Hollywood in the mid-1920s. There was
room for youth, creativity, and independence in the
movie business.

But Walt Disney was simply too young and
inexperienced to walk into Hollywood and become a
director. The only work that he found was as an extra on
horseback in a cavalry movie.

The movie business appeared closed to him, and soon he was again running low on money. He had given up on cartoon animation, and now he was failing in the motion picture business. Once again he turned to Roy, who was still recovering from tuberculosis at a veterans' hospital in Los Angeles.

"I think you'd better give the cartoon business another try, Walt," Roy said.

"No, I'm too late," Walt replied. "I should have started six years ago. I don't see how I can top those New York boys now."[1]

Walt knew that the cartoon business was centered in New York, but he had to make money somehow. So he unpacked his animation equipment and went to work making the same kind of advertising cartoons, with a local flavor, that he had made in Kansas City. He had trouble finding buyers, but finally sold a series to a local theater chain.

In the meantime Disney wrote to Margaret Winkler, the film distributor who had previously been interested in *Alice's Wonderland.* He informed her that he was still in business, despite the failure of Laugh-O-Grams. When Winkler returned his letter, she expressed continued interest in *Alice's Wonderland.* She reminded Disney that he had never sent her a sample of the unfinished film. He realized that he still had someone interested in his work.

Disney sent Winkler the unfinished print of the film

Playing polo kept Disney physically active while introducing him to the Hollywood social scene. Here he chats with actor Leslie Howard, famous for his role as Ashley Wilkes in *Gone With the Wind*.

and another letter, confidently announcing his intention to begin production on a series of Alice comedies. Disney hoped that the confident tone of his letter would pique the distributor's interest in his cartoons.

His strategy worked. Winkler liked *Alice's Wonderland* and agreed to distribute Disney's further Alice comedies at $1,500 for each finished film. This was the break Walt Disney had been waiting for.

Disney soon visited his brother Roy in the hospital. Careful not to awaken the other patients in the ward, the two brothers whispered as they discussed Walt's future. Roy asked Walt if he could produce the Alice films for the price Winkler was offering.

"For half that," Walt said confidently. "We'll make seven hundred fifty dollars profit on every one in the series!"

" *We?* " Roy asked.

"Yes, *we*," Walt repeated. "I can't possibly do it unless you come in with me. I need your help, Roy. You've just got to get out of here and join me. Please say you'll do it."[2]

After a night of tossing and turning, Roy agreed to go into business with his creative and ambitious brother. He checked himself out of the veterans' hospital long before the doctors believed that he was fully recovered from his tuberculosis. Despite doctors' warnings, Roy left the hospital and invested all his savings to help start the Disney Brothers' Studio. Walt Disney did all the animation himself for *Alice's Day at Sea.* He hired just two women to ink and paint the cels, tracing the guide of Walt's animation.

The Disney Brothers' Studio worked in this fashion until after the sixth Alice comedy. Then Margaret Winkler complained of the low film rentals that she was receiving for Disney's cartoons. She blamed the low rentals on her belief that the quality of animation was diminishing with each film. Winkler had earlier contracted for another six films, but now said that she would not keep that agreement because of the poor quality of the last cartoons.

Disney stood his ground. He told her that he was sticking to the contract, and so would she. He further surprised her by agreeing that the quality had worsened on the later films, because they were continually running low on money and time. Disney explained that they had gone way over budget on the seventh Alice comedy. It was a quality cartoon because they had taken the extra time and money needed to make it a quality cartoon. If she would only look at the cartoon, Disney told Winkler, she would see that he was right.

Winkler screened the cartoon and saw that the quality of animation was higher. The humor of the gags was also funnier than in the previous cartoons. She was convinced, and the Disney Brothers' Studio soon had a contract for twelve additional Alice comedies.

Winkler was happy with the Disney cartoons for the

Walt and Roy Disney formed the Disney Brothers' Studio in 1923. Disney is shown here working at his desk.

most part. But in a letter some time later, Winkler wrote, "do try to get a livelier quality into your cartoon characters. Everyone around here agrees the ideas are brilliant, but your execution lacks something."[3]

Disney knew exactly what she meant. Walt Disney had good skills as an artist and an excellent talent for storytelling. But he was not a great draftsman. He was not a great animator. Disney knew all the great animators were in New York, making professional-looking cartoons. All the great animators—except one. Ub Iwerks was still back in Kansas City, working for the Kansas City Film Ad Company. Disney knew Iwerks could give his cartoons everything they lacked, so Disney sent for him. To Disney's delight, Iwerks accepted.

Iwerks began work for what was now called the Disney Studios in the summer of 1924. His animation skills greatly elevated the quality of the next set of Alice cartoons. The cartoons were turning a good profit, and the Disney Studios, at last, was collecting some capital.

Amid the busy production of what would eventually be fifty-six Alice cartoons, Roy Disney married his longtime sweetheart from Kansas City, Edna Francis, on April 11, 1925. Walt served as Roy's best man, and Lillian Bonds was the maid of honor at the wedding. Bonds, a young woman who had recently become an inker at the studio, was the maid of honor at Walt's request. It seems Walt Disney had taken more than a casual interest in the pretty young inker.

"I never had any idea of getting involved with the boss," Lillian later said. "The guy didn't even have a sweater to take you out anyplace."[4]

As Walt and Lillian's romance developed, the distribution of the Alice cartoons was turned over to Margaret Winkler's husband Charlie Mintz. Mintz ordered eighteen more Alice cartoons at $1,800 per cartoon. Disney brought three more of his previous Kansas City animators into the Disney Studios to meet the demand, including future Bugs Bunny director Friz Freleng. Then he and Roy bought a lot on Hyperion Avenue in Los Angeles, where they planned to build a new one-story animation studio.

Walt Disney married Lillian Bonds on July 13, 1925, at the home of Lillian's uncle in Lewiston, Idaho. Lillian giggled through the entire ceremony.[5]

After their honeymoon the couple returned to a small one-room apartment near the studio. Lillian got used to the fact that her husband's life was greatly governed by his work. They often went out in the evening with the intention of eating dinner. Then Walt would tell her that he had something to do at the studio first. At the studio Walt was soon deep into his work, and Lillian was deep into sleep on his office couch. This scenario happened over and over.

Disney was impulsive about his work because he

now had more people to pay, including the child actress who played Alice in the cartoons. He could not fall behind, or he and Roy could not pay the staff. The rocky relationship with the new distributor Charlie Mintz put even more pressure on the Disney brothers.

In 1927 the head of Universal Pictures, Carl Laemmle, asked Charlie Mintz for a new cartoon series about a rabbit. The popularity of the Alice cartoons was fading, and Disney jumped at the prospect of doing something new. Walt Disney collaborated with Ub Iwerks and the other animators to create a new character named Oswald the Lucky Rabbit. To show their enthusiasm and professionalism, the artists quickly produced the first Oswald cartoon. *Poor Papa* was sent to Mintz and Universal Pictures in April 1927. After changing and refining the character to Universal's satisfaction, the Oswald cartoons were a big success. They attracted good money at the box office and won warm reviews.

In the summer of 1927 the studio's name was changed to Walt Disney Studios. The change was suggested by Roy, a humble man with little ego. He reasoned that the name change created a better link with the public by having moviegoers associate one individual—Walt—with the kind of cartoon entertainment that the studio was producing. Throughout 1927 Walt Disney Studios was cruising along on the popularity of Oswald the Lucky Rabbit, but there was trouble ahead.

Every two weeks Charlie Mintz sent his brother-in-law George Winkler to pick up the negative for the latest Oswald cartoon. Walt and Roy Disney were unaware that Winkler's talks with the animators during these visits were not just casual conversations. Disney had been driving his animators hard, and was still unable to pay them highly for the hard work and long hours that they put in at the studio.[6] Only when the time came to renew the contract for the Oswald cartoons did Walt discover what had been happening between Winkler and the animators.

Walt and Lillian Disney traveled to New York to renegotiate the distribution contract with Mintz. Following a friendly talk over lunch, Disney and Mintz returned to Mintz's office, where Mintz dropped the bombshell. Disney's advance per cartoon would be cut from $2,250 to $1,800. If this offer was not acceptable to the Disney studio, Mintz told Disney that he would produce the Oswald cartoons himself—using Walt's animators to do it.[7]

Disney was stunned to realize that the successful Oswald character could be taken from him that easily.[8] Although Walt Disney Studios produced the cartoons, Universal Pictures owned the copyright to the Oswald character. Now Mintz informed Disney that if he did not accept the new terms, most of the Disney animators were prepared to leave the studio and come to New York to produce the Oswald cartoons for Mintz's distribution company.

Disney made several calls to California, in which Roy confirmed Universal's ownership of the Oswald character and the likely departure of most of Disney's animators. This posed a huge threat to the financial future of the studio. Roy told Walt that he had little choice but to accept the terms of Mintz's new contract. But Roy believed that they could still save the studio by creating another cartoon character—their *own* character.

Disney again met with Mintz and accepted the new terms. Later he and Lillian boarded a train for the long trip back to California. The trip to New York had been a nightmarish disaster for his studio, but while riding the train across the country toward California, Disney began gearing his imagination toward Roy's idea of creating a new character.

As the train drew him across the countryside, Disney began to think of a little round-eared mouse. A funny little mouse full of mischief and good cheer. What would he name such a mouse?

5

The Talking Mouse

Walt Disney returned home in March 1928 with the idea for a new character still brewing in his head. The problem was how to get the character animated and into a cartoon. There were three more Oswald cartoons to produce, and after they were completed, most of the Disney animators were heading to New York to work for Charlie Mintz. The Walt Disney Studio was now basically in the employ of Charlie Mintz until the Oswald contract was completed.

If the studio did not have a new character created, animated, and ready to be shown in theaters when the contract was up, the studio risked failing. Disney and Ub Iwerks would have to make the cartoon in secret.

First, Disney described the mouse character and made sketches of how he envisioned its shape, movement, and visual personality. Disney no longer did the actual animation at the studio. Instead he entrusted Iwerks to give the character life and movement with his natural flare for animation. Many names were suggested for the character, including Mortimer Mouse. Somewhere, amid brainstorms with Iwerks and suggestions from Roy and Lillian, Walt decided to call the character Mickey Mouse.[1]

While the defecting animators worked on the Oswald cartoons, Iwerks did the animation drawings in a locked room at the studio. He hid the drawings, replacing them with Oswald sketches, whenever someone asked to enter. The rest of the animation process was much harder to hide within the studio. They could not use the camera or the studio's animation cels without the other animators discovering what they were up to.

To complete the animation, Walt had to construct a makeshift animation workshop in his garage. Walt's wife Lillian, Roy's wife Edna, and Walt's sister-in-law Hazel Sewell completed the inking and painting on cels of Ub's animation for the first cartoon, entitled *Plane Crazy*. Disney and Iwerks had cooked up its story line from the recent excitement surrounding Charles Lindbergh's historic first solo airplane flight across the Atlantic.

At night Disney and a loyal employee, Mike Marcus, took the completed cels to the studio and used the camera to complete the animation. When they were finished, all evidence of their using the camera for the "non-Oswald" cartoon was cleaned up and removed. So while Charlie Mintz "used" Walt Disney Studios to produce Oswald cartoons, Disney used the time to produce the first Mickey Mouse cartoon—in total secrecy.

Disney previewed the Mickey Mouse cartoon in May 1928 at a theater on Sunset Boulevard. He slipped the theater organist a dollar so that the cartoon gags would be punched over appropriately with music. Its reception was no sensation, but good enough to get Walt enthused and busy on the second Mickey Mouse cartoon, *The Gallopin' Gaucho.*

Walt Disney Studios was a different place by then. The contract with Mintz was completed, and the animators who had originally threatened to defect had gone to animate Oswald for Mintz in New York. The studio now consisted of only Walt and Roy Disney, Ub Iwerks, three other animators, three inkers, and the janitor. And, of course, Mickey Mouse.

Disney's next challenge was to find a new distributor for the two Mickey Mouse cartoons. Major movie studios such as MGM owned chains of movie theaters across the country in which to show their films. But the major studios were not interested in distributing his cartoons. "[They're] very nice," the studio executives told Walt. "There's only one trouble. Nobody's ever heard of Mickey Mouse."[2]

Of course they had never heard of Mickey Mouse.

Mickey's cartoons had no distributor! But the remark turned out to be rather ironic.

Audiences may not have heard of Mickey Mouse, but they were starting, literally, to *hear* the movies. The first sound motion picture *The Jazz Singer*, starring Al Jolsen, had premiered a few months earlier in New York City on October 6, 1927. Some thought that sound pictures were merely a passing fad. They doubted that theater-owners across the country would make the investment of wiring their theaters for sound. But others, including Walt Disney, believed that sound movies were the wave of the future in the movie business. Disney and others clearly saw that the addition of sound would revolutionize the storytelling potential of motion pictures.

Although the process of talking motion pictures, or "talkies," was not yet perfected, Disney believed that audiences would find it highly entertaining to *hear* Mickey Mouse. Walt was sure of one thing: if he could make it work, the first sound cartoon, starring Mickey Mouse, would be a sensation.[3]

Disney and his animators quickly came up with the story line for a third Mickey Mouse cartoon called *Steamboat Willie*. The story line was conceived with the expectation that the animation would somehow match the sound with the on-screen action, such as when Mickey used the udders, teeth, and tails of barnyard animals as musical instruments to play the tune of "Turkey in the Straw."

Disney and another animator, Wilfred Jackson, figured out a way to time the animation to the music. Knowing that film passed through the camera at twenty-four frames per second, Disney counted the time as Jackson played the tune on his harmonica. Then he calculated how many frames of cartoon would be required to match the beats of the music. So when Mickey hopped up and down while whistling a tune at the wheel of his steamboat, the animators knew how many frames to make him go up and how many to make him go down—exactly in rhythm with the song.

On a warm night in July 1928, Disney gathered his staff and their wives to witness a test of the completed animation. Roy Disney operated the camera from outside the window to reduce the noise from the projector sprockets. Walt, Wilfred Jackson, Johnny Cannon, and Ub Iwerks stood in front of a microphone behind a bedsheet-screen, providing the voices, music, and sound effects for the film. The overall impression with their homemade sound effects was crude, but the timing process seemed to work. Now Disney needed to find a high-quality system to affix a recording to the film. Then he would need real musicians, real sound effects, and real voices to record the actual soundtrack.

Disney headed for New York early in the fall of 1928, intending to find a way to add sound to *Steamboat Willie*. The movie industry was still not convinced of the future of sound motion pictures, so his search for a dependable sound system was a difficult one. After more than a week of searching, Disney spent the afternoon with a man named Pat Powers. Powers owned an independent movie sound system called Cinephone. Disney signed with Powers for the use of the system, giving him a $500 deposit. Then he spent the next weeks putting together a recording session.

The first session was an expensive disaster. The seventeen-piece orchestra never matched the speed of the action on the film, but the second session was a success, and Disney was sure he had a hit on his hands. Powers arranged for Disney to show the cartoon at the offices of the major film distributors. The distributors all liked the cartoon, but showed little enthusiasm for it and no intention of investing their money to distribute it.

Disney thought *Steamboat Willie* was a surefire hit. He did not understand the distributors' apathy toward it. Then a man named Harry Reichenbach told him that the distributors had a poor sense for what the public wanted.[4]

Reichenbach ran the Colony Theater in New York City. He offered Disney $1,000 to show the cartoon for two weeks with the rest of the theater's films. Disney badly needed the money to offset the high costs of the recording sessions, and Reichenbach convinced him that the public and the movie reviewers would come to his theater in droves to see "the FIRST animated cartoon with SOUND."[5]

Disney agreed, and Reichenbach's strategy worked.

Steamboat Willie opened at the Colony Theater on November 18, 1928. For days after, the New York crowds rolled in to see *and hear* Mickey Mouse. Walt Disney had scored a hit with audiences and film critics alike. As he had fully expected, the frolicking and *talking* Mickey Mouse was an entertainment sensation. On top of it all, Disney himself had provided the voice for Mickey's little actual dialogue.

Disney struck a deal to distribute the cartoons through Pat Powers, who wanted simultaneously to promote his Cinephone sound process. The future looked bright. But when Walt returned to California, Roy blew his top. He had discovered a clause in their contract with Powers that stated that the studio would pay Powers $26,000 a year for the use of his sound equipment. Walt and Roy had an argument over the contract, ending with Walt's insistence that he needed the equipment to do the cartoons.[6]

The Walt Disney Studios expanded with new animators to produce more antics starring Mickey Mouse. Mickey's popularity was growing with each new cartoon. Disney had a deep affection for Mickey, a character so full of Walt's personality that the Disney animators began to see Mickey as Walt's boyish alter ego. Walt had provided Mickey's voice at the suggestion of the original recording people in New York—after no one else's voice had seemed suitable. And somehow, like everything Disney did for Mickey, it was just right.

The popularity of Mickey Mouse was phenomenal. Newspapers
carried this picture of Walt Disney with a figure of his famous
mouse as he boarded an airplane for a visit to the Chicago World's
Fair in 1933.

Mickey's popularity with movie audiences had become a national phenomenon by the end of 1929. The squeaky voice Walt supplied Mickey had become the most recognizable voice in America.[7] When audiences filed out of theaters, they were more often talking about the exploits of Mickey and Minnie Mouse than about the adventures of the hero in the feature attraction.

Mickey Mouse was a big star. Yet Walt Disney did not want to be limited to making cartoons always starring the same character. Despite Mickey's popularity, Disney knew—from his experience with the Alice comedies—that Mickey's possibilities would eventually run dry. The studio had to expand and diversify if it wanted to survive financially and artistically.

Disney's creative vision was by no means limited to producing a continuous series of Mickey Mouse cartoons. Walt envisioned something far more ambitious. He was seeking to revolutionize the entire field of animated cartoons.

Such a goal would have to be accomplished in steps. Disney's first step was to start a new series of cartoons called *Silly Symphonies*. Each cartoon would have a different subject, with no continuous characters. This gave Disney and his animators room to try different artistic techniques. They could also experiment with new camera and sound equipment that would enhance the impact of the animated images. The first of these cartoons, *The Skeleton Dance*, was a musical cartoon

For his work in creating the Mickey Mouse and *Silly Symphonies* cartoons, Walt Disney received a special award in 1937 from the Academy of Motion Picture Arts & Sciences for excellence in the field of animation.

featuring skeletons humorously dancing and twirling through a cemetery on a moonlit night.

Pat Powers only wanted Mickey Mouse, and claimed that he could not sell the Halloween-spirited cartoon to any theaters. But after Walt premiered it himself at a Hollywood theater, where audiences enjoyed the dancing bone show, Powers agreed to distribute it to theaters. Critics hailed the quality and inventiveness of the *Silly Symphonies*, and Disney soon had another successful cartoon series on his hands.

But success in the animated cartoon business was deceptive. The costs of the animation experiments involved in producing the *Silly Symphonies* ran high. The Mickey Mouse cartoons were bringing in good profits, but the studio was financially strained by its contractual agreement to pay Powers for the use of the Cinephone sound equipment. The strain was pressuring Disney to drive his animators hard again—harder than some of them could tolerate. A few, including his old friend Ub Iwerks, were thinking about leaving.

By 1930, though Mickey Mouse was a huge success, the cost of animation and the contract with Powers were driving the studio toward bankruptcy again. And the stress and strain of keeping the studio afloat was pushing Walt Disney toward a nervous breakdown.[8]

6

Creating a World for Seven Dwarfs

In January 1930, Disney watched as his world unraveled before his eyes.

Walt and Roy Disney were dissatisfied with Pat Powers' reports of theater royalties owed the Disney studio. When Disney traveled to New York and confronted Powers, Powers denied everything. Then, to make clear that he was in a commanding position to control affairs with the studio, Powers revealed a surprise. He had offered Ub Iwerks the chance to leave Disney and start his own animation studio. Powers boasted that Iwerks was already prepared to resign.

Disney telephoned Iwerks in California and made a desperate effort to convince his old friend to stay with the studio. But Iwerks was set on starting his own studio with Powers. The situation was an utter disaster. Disney had little choice but to break with Powers, whom Disney claimed still owed him $150,000 in unpaid theater royalties. He had lost his best animator, and the right to use the Cinephone sound system was taken from Disney and given to Iwerks.

That was not the end of Disney's problems. Powers was a feared man in Hollywood. So whenever Disney attempted to find a new distributor, Powers threatened some distributors Disney contacted with lawsuits, since the contract still gave Powers exclusive rights to Disney's films.[1]

Walt and Roy Disney were hemmed in on every side. Then they met with Harry Cohn, the president of Columbia Pictures. Cohn was not at all afraid of Powers and was eager to sign an agreement to distribute the popular Disney cartoons. When Powers sued as expected, Cohn responded by hiring a team of top New York lawyers. Cohn then had the lawyers draw up countersuit papers. These papers were hand-delivered to Powers by some broad-shouldered fellows who had the intimidating appearance of gangster henchmen. Powers quickly decided to let Cohn buy out his Disney contract for $50,000.

The studio was saved for the moment, but another crisis hit when Powers lured away Disney's talented musical director Carl Stalling. The studio could function without Iwerks and Stalling, but the losses were a blow, if only temporarily, to the studio's creative and artistic quality.

The strain of saving the studio from ruin had pushed Walt's emotions to the limit. The stress had weighed heavily on him, and he felt deeply and personally betrayed by his old friend Ub Iwerks. His mood grew increasingly dark as he and Lillian left New York on the train for California.[2] During the months after his return home, he worked feverishly, taking sleeping pills to get to sleep. His emotions were on edge, and he grew deeply depressed.[3]

He was further troubled by his continued longing for a child. Walt and Lillian had been trying during their four years of marriage to have a baby, but Lillian had yet to become pregnant. When a doctor assured Lillian that she was not to blame, the implication created a feeling of inadequacy as a man in Walt. This feeling deepened even further when Roy and his wife had their first child, Roy Edward Disney, in January 1930. Some have suggested that Walt's creation of Mickey Mouse and his affection for the character were partly due to his desire to compensate for being childless.[4] Finally, one evening Lillian found Walt collapsed in their bedroom. Disney later said:

> I guess I was working too hard and worrying too much. . . . In 1931 I had a nervous breakdown. . . . I couldn't sleep. I reached the point when I couldn't even talk over the telephone without crying. I was in a highly emotional state.[5]

Lillian dismissed his doctor's suggestion that Walt be hospitalized. The doctor insisted that, at the very least, Walt must take a complete break of several weeks from the pressures of the studio, which had driven him to the emotional collapse. Walt greatly needed an extended vacation with lots of rest, the doctor said.

Walt and Lillian took the doctor's advice. They and another couple soon left on a two-month vacation that took them to Washington, D.C., New Orleans, New York, and down the Atlantic coast to Florida. Next they boarded a cruise ship to Cuba, then headed to Panama and through the Panama Canal before finally returning along the Pacific coast to California by private yacht. When Walt returned home he was his old self again. His complete recovery was clear to everyone at the studio. Their boss was again filled with the enthusiasm to try something new—cartoons in color.

During Walt's absence, Roy had changed the distribution of Disney cartoons by signing a new contract with United Artists. Now Walt wanted United Artists to support him in making color cartoons through the new color film processing technique called Technicolor.

"We'd be crazy to take on the expense of color just after we've made a deal with United Artists," Roy argued. "They won't advance us any more money for color."[6]

Walt countered that color cartoons would excite the

public and give the films longer playdates and bigger rentals. Roy told Walt that the studio would not see that money for years and that they were already deeply in debt. Besides, Roy added, colored paints might not stick to the cel or would later chip off.

Walt insisted that they try to develop paints that would do the job. The color process was to be tried on a Silly Symphony cartoon called *Flowers and Trees*, a nature cartoon featuring animated plants dancing to the flow of classical music. Disney and his lab technicians worked night and day to develop paints that did not chip when dry and did not fade under the hot lights. After many failures, they developed a set of stable colors that successfully adhered to the cels. Disney's studio had now opened the door for color cartoons.

Flowers and Trees opened in July 1932, creating the sensation that Disney had hoped for as well as raising both the popularity and respectability of the *Silly Symphonies* cartoons. All future *Silly Symphonies* were to be in color and animated with a high standard of quality and creativity. With the *Silly Symphonies* and the phenomenally popular Mickey Mouse cartoons on the production schedule, the staff at Walt Disney Productions increased to over seventy.

Walt was already investing in the future of his artists. In 1931 he had arranged with the Chouinard Art Institute in Los Angeles for his artists to take night classes there. When more money flowed in as the studio began to benefit from the United Artists contract, Walt established an art school at the studio. He asked one of the Chouinard teachers to conduct the class two nights a week in the studio's sound stage.

There was a plan to all of this. Disney had already introduced sound and color to the world of animation, but he envisioned so much more. If he could further develop the talents of his artists and technicians, his studio could push the artistic limits of animated entertainment to heights no one else imagined at that time. The school was part of that plan. The artists, technicians, musicians, and Walt himself were constantly learning.

Amid all the hustle and bustle at the studio, Mickey Mouse won an Oscar. In November 1932, the Academy of Motion Picture Arts and Sciences awarded Disney a special Oscar for the creation of Mickey Mouse. Disney also won an Oscar for *Flowers and Trees,* the Academy's first award to a cartoon. But Mickey Mouse was still the star. His fame had grown worldwide, and sales of Mickey Mouse merchandise were bringing in handsome sums to the studio. Walt maintained his connection with Mickey's warm and fun-loving character. Whenever the writers and animators overstepped the limits or simplicity of Mickey's character, Walt was quick to say, "Remember, he's just a mouse."[7]

Disney triumphed again in 1933 with the release of the thirty-sixth *Silly Symphonies,* titled *Three Little Pigs.*

Never before had Disney's animated characters come so strongly to life on the screen. The combination of sound, color, and music in the cartoon was the best yet from the Disney studio. The effects added extra dimensions to the characters of the Three Pigs and the Big Bad Wolf. The cartoon was tremendously popular, playing in theaters week after week.

Apparently the entertaining cartoon struck a chord with the millions of Americans suffering through the Great Depression in the 1930s. The song "Who's Afraid of the Big Bad Wolf?" became the most popular song in the country. It was a sort of rallying cry to those struggling daily through the Depression to "keep the wolf from the door."[8]

Disney had not expected the huge success of *Three Little Pigs*. But around the same time as its release, he got an even bigger surprise. His wife Lillian was pregnant.

On December 18, 1933, Lillian gave birth to Diane Marie Disney. Walt Disney was at last a happy father.[9] He would spend the rest of her childhood resisting the temptation to spoil her.

Walt was now happier and even busier at the studio.[10] The Disney studios at its new location on Hyperion Avenue employed two hundred people by the end of 1934, and it continued to expand. Donald Duck, Minnie Mouse, Pluto, and Goofy were added to the stable of animated stars. The characters further increased the demand for Disney cartoons. By the fall of 1934,

Disney's *Three Little Pigs* achieved new heights for combining animation technique, character, and music into an animated cartoon. Disney, at left, listens to the voices of the Three Pigs, from left to right, Dorothy Compton, Pinto Colvig, and Mary Moder.

Disney decided that it was time for the studio to expand in a new direction. The training and schooling of existing artists and the hiring of new ones was continuing, and Disney was now ready to focus them on a new and ambitious project.

It began when his chief animators returned to the studio after dinner one night at a cafe across the street from the studio. Disney told them to come into the sound stage because he had something to tell them. There, for the next two hours, the animators listened to Walt. He described and acted out the fairy tale story for what he envisioned as the first animated feature film *Snow White and the Seven Dwarfs*.[11]

The animation project was of staggering proportions, and some of the animators thought that the idea was crazy, but before long Disney's enthusiasm for the project had spread throughout the studio. The story, animation, and music departments at the studio would have to work closer than ever before to pull together the elements of such a film—to create an entertaining and dramatic whole. Disney was already a pioneer in animation. His goal now was to top himself, and push the art of animation to a new level.

Snow White and the Seven Dwarfs went into production for the next three years, pushing the studio's people and financial resources to the limit. Much of its production involved breaking new ground.

Music was to be an integral part of the story. As

many as twenty-five different songs were written, tried, and rejected before finally settling on the songs that made it into the film. Hundreds of long sessions were held with story people and animators to create the right appearance and personality for each character.

Animators were assigned individual scenes. Each scene was mapped out in meticulous detail with regard to the movements, mannerisms, and expressions of the characters before being animated. The right voices had to be found for each character, including the voice of the Magic Mirror and the musical whistling and warbling of the birds. Pinto Colvig, who did the voice for Goofy in Disney cartoons, did double duty on the film as the voice of both Grumpy and Sneezy.

A few scenes in the film were to have a striking appearance never before seen in animation. Disney and his technicians were developing a large device called the multiplane camera. This camera apparatus, which stood more than ten meters (thirty feet) high, was capable of shooting through several different layers of cels on glass panes. It could move forward and backward, creating a sense of movement within a scene and a greater feeling of depth, or three-dimensional perspective.

With the use of this camera, foregrounds and backgrounds could be made more elaborate. For example, a "blurring" effect could give the impression of flowing water in a stream or the vague red glow around a fire. These were effects that could never be achieved with a flat conventional animation cel alone. The new effects gave audiences the feeling that they were watching a three-dimensional world instead of a flat drawing in motion.[12]

In 1937 production moved into its third year, with the film starting to take impressive shape. Besides the artistic quality and technical wizardry of the developing picture, the core of the film's success lay in its ability to tell a good story. The story was immeasurably helped by Disney's keen observation that Snow White and the Prince were actually the least interesting of all the characters in the story. Yet they were the lead characters in the fairy tale and could not be relegated to supporting roles. The answer was to intertwine the actions of Snow White, the Prince, and the Queen very subtly with the comedy of the Dwarfs—whose personalities were far more interesting.

"We care more about what happens to Snow White," said one movie observer, "because the Dwarfs—far more vivid personalities than she—care so much for her, and much of the comedy arises from their concern."[13]

The years and expense that went into the risky project caused some to call it "Disney's Folly." Many believed audiences' attention could not be held throughout a feature-length cartoon with a fully developed plot. Others suggested that audiences would not tolerate so many bright colors on the screen for so long. But they did not understand or perceive the revolutionary leap forward in animated storytelling that *Snow White and the Seven Dwarfs* represented.

Disney finally viewed the completed film in the fall of 1937. He was pleased, but his eye for detail saw a disturbing defect at the film's climax, when the Prince bends down to kiss Snow White. A problem with the camerawork caused the animated Prince to shimmy slightly. Disney wanted the defect fixed, a repair that would cost thousands of dollars or more.

This time Roy Disney put his foot down. Roy told Walt that the studio was already deeply in debt to the Bank of America, and that they absolutely would *not* make such an expensive repair to an already finished film. "Let the Prince shimmy," Roy said. And the Prince shimmies to this day.[14]

Snow White and the Seven Dwarfs premiered December 21, 1937, at the Carthay Circle Theater in Hollywood. Audiences flocked to the theaters and were spellbound by the magical world Disney and his people had created on the screen. Many reviewers immediately hailed the film as a masterpiece. Walt's fame grew to near-legendary stature. At age thirty-seven, his place in motion picture history and his reputation as an innovative genius were assured.

Snow White and the Seven Dwarfs surpassed all Disney's expectations. In its first run it played to more than twenty million theater-goers. It also earned more

Child actress Shirley Temple presented Walt Disney with special "Oscars" at the 1938 Academy Awards Ceremony. To honor his work on *Snow White and the Seven Dwarfs,* the Academy of Motion Picture Arts & Sciences presented him with a special trophy of one large Oscar and seven smaller Oscars, one for each of the seven dwarfs.

than $8 million at a time when the average ticket price was twenty-five cents. "Disney's Folly," as it had been called by doubters, earned twice as much money as any other film up to that time! At the 1938 Academy Awards, Walt was given one full-sized Oscar and seven little Oscars (one for each dwarf) for the film that had "charmed and pioneered a great new entertainment field for the motion picture cartoon."[15]

By using animation to create a colorful and enchanting fantasy world, Walt Disney had scored a gigantic triumph in producing the first animated feature film. But the creative zeal within Disney never allowed him to rest on his success. With the completion of *Snow White and the Seven Dwarfs*, there were now new films to produce and new worlds to create.

7

The Strike, the War, and the Glass Slipper

The success of *Snow White and the Seven Dwarfs* was not Disney's only source of happiness as 1938 progressed. After daughter Diane's birth in 1933, more difficulties in bearing their own children made Walt and Lillian decide to adopt. Amid the busy rush of producing *Snow White* in January 1937, two-week-old Sharon Mae Disney had arrived at the Disney home, welcomed by a very loving family.

"We weren't raised with the idea that this is a great man," said Sharon Disney. "He was Daddy. He went to work every morning. He came home every night."[1]

Walt Disney, being very much a child at heart, had to resist the temptation to shower his girls with toys and games. Somehow Walt and Lillian managed never to spoil their daughters. Although in later years Diane

Disney still claimed, "Daddy is a pushover. He's the biggest softie in the world."[2]

In the midst of this happiness and success, tragedy struck in November 1938. Walt and Roy's mother Flora died from fumes that leaked from the gas furnace in their home near Los Angeles. Disney's father Elias also suffered from the mishap, but survived. Elias Disney grew very withdrawn in his remaining years, and was never quite the same after Flora's death. Despite the tragic accident, Walt and Roy continued their work at the studio, moving at a fast pace in the aftermath of *Snow White*'s success.

By the end of 1938, in addition to the Mickey Mouse cartoons and the *Silly Symphonies*, three more feature films were in various stages of production. *Pinocchio*, the story of a marionette who wants to become a boy, was the priority project—most likely to be produced first. Also in production were *Fantasia*, a new kind of film in which Walt hoped to meld animation and classical music into a different type of entertainment experience, and *Bambi*, the story of a young deer.

All three presented opportunities to break new ground in animation technique. Use of the multiplane camera had been nearly perfected. So while its use was limited in *Snow White and the Seven Dwarfs*, it was used nearly throughout in *Pinocchio*. Disney animators were greatly challenged to give warmth and personality to a character who was essentially a wooden puppet. Eventually Pinocchio's features were rounded and his movements enlivened to Disney's satisfaction.

Bambi presented the challenge of animating animal characters with movements that looked realistic. *Fantasia* was another experiment entirely. The animators were asked to listen to famous pieces of classical music and then imagine how to draw what they heard. One piece of music inspired animators to do a segment about the creation of Earth and the age of dinosaurs. Another piece inspired a story about the Greek gods.

Disney plowed much of the profits from *Snow White* into building a plush new studio on Buena Vista Street in Burbank, California. The completed studio cost $3 million. Many of Disney's animators, who felt they had never been paid fairly for their hard work on *Snow White*, wondered why the money went into the new studio instead of higher employee salaries.[3]

By the end of 1939, the shining success of *Snow White* was beginning to dim. As the Nazis swarmed Europe at the beginning of World War II, foreign markets representing nearly half of the studio's income disappeared. The drying up of funds came at a time when all three feature-film projects were behind schedule and expenses were mounting.

Pinocchio eventually opened in theaters in February 1940. It received rave reviews and did good business in the United States, but the loss of foreign markets hurt the film. It failed to recover its $2.6 million production cost on its first release to theaters.

Disney suffered an even bigger loss in 1940 with *Fantasia*. While the film was visually exciting, its full impact was hampered by theaters' resistance to install elaborate sound systems for the classical music score. Many moviegoers simply did not understand what the film was. The lack of a connected story line and the fact that many people felt that the classical music was too snobbish kept audiences away.

The studio was now $4.5 million in debt. *Bambi*, the next feature, was proving an expensively slow picture to make, and could not be rushed into theaters to bring in money to the studio. Many of the studio's workers already believed that they were overworked and underpaid when rumors started circulating that they were going to be laid off.

Instead of laying off employees, Walt and Roy Disney sold stock in the company at $25 a share. The sale brought in enough money to keep the company afloat. One-fifth of the stock was issued to Disney employees, but as the stock price fell, some of the employees sold their shares. This was done partly because they had little confidence in the studio's future and partly because their pay from the studio gave them little money to spend beyond their living expenses.

The financial situation at the studio was becoming critical. An effort was made to economize some of their projects to get them into the theaters more quickly. *Dumbo*, a story about a flying elephant, was to be a feature film at just over sixty minutes. It was to contain straight animation and few, if any, special effects. The film looked like it would be good, but the studio's main objective at this critical stage was to make it *profitable.*

The problems between Disney and his studio workers, now numbering fifteen hundred, came to a head in May 1941. When Disney could not ease the growing tension and dissatisfaction of many of his overworked employees, a union came in and organized a strike. Walt and Roy Disney made no concessions to the strikers. Walt believed that the strike would last only days. After several weeks passed with no real movement from the studio, the strike turned ugly.

Strikers set up a picket line across from the studio. They carried signs with nasty slogans and hurled angry words at Disney when he arrived for work. The strike was mostly the result of unfortunate misunderstandings. Disney mistakenly believed that his younger animators and staffers did not need higher pay. And the strikers mistakenly believed that Walt was rolling in wealth from the profits of the studio's films.

Nevertheless, Walt Disney was hurt to the core by the strike.[4] Again he believed his co-workers, to whom he felt such loyalty, had betrayed him. During the most bitter part of the strike, Disney finally agreed to a request from the United States State Department to make a goodwill trip to South America. There, he and a handpicked staff were to shoot film for a movie called *The Three Caballeros*. The movie was a mixture of Disney animation and footage about the people and places of South America.

Roy Disney managed to settle the strike during Walt's absence by agreeing that the studio would recognize the Cartoonists Guild. Walt had to accept the settlement, realizing that the nature of the animation business in Hollywood had forever changed. Thereafter, all Disney facilities would be unionized.

Walt also learned during his trip that his father Elias Disney had died. He later returned to California full of guilt that he had not been present for his father's funeral or with him during his last days.[5]

The months after his return, in the wake of the strike, were a dark time for Walt Disney. The strike had changed the relationship between him and his employees. Several striking animators were entitled by law to be given back their jobs. But their creative cartooning careers were essentially ended by a vengeful Walt Disney, who sent no work in their direction. It was a tense and uncomfortable time for everyone at the studio.

Dumbo opened in theaters on Halloween of 1941. The humble little movie proved to be immensely popular with audiences and a financial success for the studio. The expensive *Bambi* was still not ready for release.

On December 7, 1941, the United States Naval base at Pearl Harbor, Hawaii, was attacked by Japanese planes—destroying much of the United States Pacific Fleet. That same afternoon Disney got a call from his studio manager. The manager said that the Army had called to inform him that five hundred soldiers were preparing to move into the studio.

The Army unit took over the large Disney studio because of its size and capability to accommodate a large number of soldiers. The unit supported anti-aircraft installations in the mountains around Los Angeles, and the studio made a perfect home for its soldiers. Shortly after the United States officially entered the war, the Navy contracted with Disney to produce twenty short films on aircraft identification. Other contracts for training and information films followed.

Bambi was finally released to theaters in August 1942. It was one of Disney's most beautiful animated films, and one of Walt's personal favorites. But its untimely release during the nation's preoccupation with the war effort dealt a huge blow to the film's business. The extremely costly *Bambi* was another huge Disney loss in its first release to theaters.[6]

The Army unit moved out of the studio after eight months, when the threat of a Japanese invasion seemed unlikely. Disney continued to produce government training films for the war effort, rather enjoying the task of interpreting complex subjects in an entertaining way.

Disney characters appealed to children around the world. To lessen children's fears during a trip to the hospital, this special ambulance in Blackpool, England, was decorated inside and out with Disney characters.

The studio made little money from the government contracts, and Disney's staff was too busy meeting the government's demands to devote time to more commercial projects. During the war, preparations for *Peter Pan* and *Alice in Wonderland* had to be abandoned.

Disney also lost money on his artists' designs for more than fourteen hundred identification patches for different military units. The designs for the patches were done at an average cost to the studio of $25 apiece. Walt never complained. "I had to do it," he said afterward. "Those kids grew up on Mickey Mouse. I owed it to 'em."[7]

When the war finally ended in 1945, the studio was rather gutted. It was now more than $4 million in debt to the Bank of America and had no big money-maker looming on its horizon. Roy Disney balked at Walt's plans to resume production on *Peter Pan* and *Alice in Wonderland*. Both promised to be expensive projects at a time when the studio could not possibly go further into debt.

To get the studio back on a good financial footing, Disney produced the studio's first live-action films—*Song of the South* and *So Dear to My Heart*. *Song of the South*, a retelling of some of the Uncle Remus tales, featured some animated segments as well as segments of combined live-action and animation. *So Dear to My Heart* was a musical movie about a pioneer family and starred actor-singer Burl Ives. Both films made little money.

The pleasant surprise to the studio during the late 1940s was the popularity of a series of nature films entitled *True-Life Adventures*. *Seal Island* and *Beaver Valley* were popular with audiences and encouraged Disney to invest in employing nature photographers to film further *True-Life Adventures*.

Soon the collection of nature films started bringing in enough money to lessen the studio's debt to the Bank of America. The money also bolstered Walt and Roy's confidence about investing in more expensive projects that would hopefully be more profitable. In late 1948 Disney started production in England on a lavish live-action version of *Treasure Island*. Production resumed in the animation departments on *Peter Pan* and *Alice in Wonderland*. Production also began on a third animated feature *Cinderella*. Because of its strong story and its similarities to *Snow White*, *Cinderella* took top priority. It was first in line to make it to the theaters. So Disney immersed himself in its production, taking part in every story meeting.

In 1949 Walt and Lillian Disney bought a new house, where Walt planned to indulge in some of his hobbies and interests—namely trains. Disney had maintained a nostalgic interest in trains ever since his days as a news butcher on the Pacific Railroad. Now he took great amusement in building a half-mile circle of track around the property of his home. The track was designed for a special scale-model train large enough for an adult to ride atop. The model train engine that he and his men in the studio's machine shop eventually built was steam-driven. It was powerful enough to pull Disney and a number of visitors around the grounds of his new home.

His interest in trains, miniatures, and other hobby amusements seemed to give him a great deal of pleasure and was a welcome relief from the pressures of the studio. Unknown to everyone around him, his small interests at home were inspiring big ideas at work.[8]

Cinderella appeared in theaters in March 1950 and was the biggest success artistically and financially for the studio since *Snow White and the Seven Dwarfs*. It was a smash hit and rekindled enthusiasm at the studio for producing quality animated features. The live-action *Treasure Island* was released later in the year and was also a big hit.

Alice in Wonderland hit the screens in 1951. The nature of its story, which Disney characterized as a little girl in a lunatic asylum, robbed the film of the engaging human charm of other Disney animated features. It did lackluster business in theaters. *Peter Pan*, a more interesting and exciting animated film that was finally released in 1953, did much better.

Disney had been having visions of a new kind of theme park for years. His tinkering with his model train and miniatures as well as his visits to other theme parks with his daughters had sparked his imagination. His

A nervous Kathryn Beaumont, who provided the voice for Alice in
Disney's *Alice in Wonderland*, stayed close to Walt Disney during
the film's world premiere in London in 1951.

mind turned toward a new creative ambition. Possibilities seemed to be opening. Money was rolling into the studio again, and there was the new medium of television.

To Walt Disney, television looked like a gold mine. It would be a new way to help make his films more popular. It would also prepare the public for what he planned to call Disneyland.

8

Disneyland

In the days before World War II began, Disney had considered the idea of building a small amusement park across the street from the studio. Disney thought that his employees could use it to unwind. He also thought that visitors could come and enjoy pony rides and train rides—all decorated with Disney characters. A lack of money and the coming of war prevented the project from ever starting, but Disney never forgot his idea for an amusement park.

His travels took him around the world, and he often visited other amusement parks with his daughters. Most were geared only to children, with little to attract or entertain adults. The parks were usually dirty, and the food was of very questionable quality. Disney saw no reason that amusement parks had to be this way. He

Walt Disney's family arrives by train in New York prior to sailing on the *Queen Elizabeth* for a vacation in 1949. From left to right are wife Lillian, daughters Sharon and Diane, and Walt.

later visited the Tivoli Gardens in Copenhagen, Denmark. There, he was impressed by the sparkling rides, the quality of the food, the affordable admission price, and the cleanliness of the entire park.

"Now this is what an amusement place should be!" he said to Lillian.[1] The visit proved to him that the idea he had been formulating in his head for years could be done.

Building the custom-made model train at his home and visiting other parks had given him many ideas. The studio had also been involved in building elaborate displays for some special exhibitions and traveling shows. All these experiences rolled together to convince Walt Disney that he could build a new kind of amusement park that would capture the imagination of people young and old.

Roy Disney refused to let Walt invest the studio's finances on such a risky and expensive venture. But Walt knew what he wanted and would not be stopped. In December 1952 he invested his own life savings and borrowed $100,000 against his life insurance to start Walt Disney, Incorporated. The company was later called WED Enterprises, which stood for Walter Elias Disney. The new firm consisted of artists, designers, architects, and engineers who were to work with Walt in developing ideas for an amusement park. Walt wanted the park to be beautiful, functional, and technically far in advance of any other amusement park in the world.

Walt later hired the Stanford Research Institute to conduct surveys and studies in order to find a suitable location for such a park. The Institute finally recommended an area of Anaheim, California. There, the climate was good and plenty of land was available for development, with access to the freeway system.[2]

Now, Walt Disney ran into a familiar problem. His dream was going to cost millions of dollars, and neither he nor his studio had millions of dollars to spend. The new medium of television, which Walt saw as a way to promote his movies and cartoons, could also prepare the public for his new amusement park. Television, Disney knew, could also raise millions of dollars to help build it.

Roy observed that his younger brother Walt, for the first time, was thinking about ways to raise money for his big ideas. Roy traveled to New York in 1953 to negotiate with the three major television networks on a deal for a weekly television program. Then the smallest of the three networks, ABC, struck a deal with Roy for a one-hour weekly series. The deal also included $500,000 in cash and more than $4 million in loans to be funneled toward building the park.

The interest of the television network persuaded Roy to put the studio's money behind the park as well. The pool of funds now made it possible to go ahead with plans to actually begin excavation at the site.

A happy interruption in Disney's work came when Walt's daughter Diane was married in 1954. Diane wed a football player for the University of Southern California, Ron Miller. Disney liked Miller a great deal.

In photographs of the wedding party, Disney stood on tiptoe beside his tall and husky new son-in-law.

In October of that year the Disney television show premiered. Naming it after the park he envisioned, Walt called the show *Disneyland*. The weekly show consisted of Disney cartoons, nature films, installments of a continuing story *Davy Crockett—King of the Wild Frontier*, entertaining documentaries, and Walt's own reports on the building of the Disneyland park. The show's high quality and variety of interesting elements made it a highly-rated program.

While Disney's interests in entertainment were becoming widely diverse, he continued his knack for scoring big hits at the theaters as well. The live-action version of Jules Verne's *20,000 Leagues Under the Sea* was an exciting adventure spectacle with an all-star cast including Kirk Douglas, Peter Lorre, and James Mason. The *Davy Crockett* episodes of the *Disneyland* television program were combined into a feature film that was a big success at the box office. His latest animated feature, *Lady and the Tramp*, with its fine story and beautiful animation, added to Disney's impressive list of successes in the mid-1950s.

The task of building Disneyland was not easy. Disney encountered almost every problem imaginable in making his dream park a reality. There were great difficulties in clearing the orange trees from the building site. A host of technical problems hampered progress on building the rides and other amusements. The heat and

At the 1954 Academy Awards, Walt Disney, in what became an
almost annual event, collected an armful of Oscars.

humidity also made working conditions uncomfortable. In addition, drainage problems and heavy rains often left parts of the park looking like a swamp.

There were building code problems with the Orange County building inspectors, several labor problems, and a strike by plumbers and asphalt workers. Through it all, Disney would not be dissuaded from his goal of completing a park that would be a special place for people of all ages.[3]

On July 17, 1955, the day had finally arrived for the opening of Disney's most ambitious dream yet—Disneyland. Because of all the problems in its construction, the $17 million park was not totally ready for the crowds, but Disney did not want to push back the opening date. The gate opened on time and the crowds rushed into the park. It was soon overcrowded, and long lines formed at the rides. Water pressure was low at drinking fountains and toilets, some exhibits and rides broke down or had to be closed, and even the cement was still soft in some places. Nearly everything that could have gone wrong *did* go wrong on the opening day. Many visitors complained about the problems that they encountered at the park.

Disneyland's opening day was disastrous, and Disney's critics were quick to take their jabs at Walt and his park. But the problems were soon solved—mechanical difficulties were fixed and the flow of people was improved. The initial round of bad press did not

Walt Disney realized another of his creative dreams with the opening of Disneyland. He is pictured in front of the Fantasyland Castle during the park's official opening in 1955.

keep the crowds away. Disneyland greeted its millionth visitor only seven weeks later. By then Disney's largest and most ambitious gamble had become his most impressive entertainment success. People from all over were coming to enjoy themselves at Disneyland.

Just three months after the opening of Disneyland, Walt and the studio scored yet another triumph on television. *The Mickey Mouse Club*, a variety show for children, premiered on October 3, 1955. It featured Disney cartoons and educational segments, and was hosted by a group of youngsters called the Mouseketeers.

Pretty Annette, widely grinning Bobby, and cute little Cubby were overnight celebrities to the millions of children who tuned in Monday through Friday at 5:00 P.M. Months later every child in America could sing the words to the show's theme song: "Who's the leader—of the club—that's made for you and me? M-I-C-K-E-Y M-O-U-S-E."[4] No one had ever before attempted a children's show of such high quality. Disney's producers and directors proved that it could be done in a way that was both entertaining and educational.

Over the next few years, Disney was a powerful force on television. The phenomenal popularity of the *Davy Crockett* episodes on the *Disneyland* program made it the most popular show on television. Sales of officially licensed Davy Crockett posters, wooden rifles, and especially coonskin hats brought unexpected profits into Walt Disney Productions.[5] *Disneyland* and *The Mickey*

Mouse Club remained two of the most highly rated programs throughout the late 1950s and early 1960s. Eventually *Zorro* rounded out the list of Disney's successful work for television.

It seemed that Disney was everywhere. Since the early 1930s—and the first appearance of Mickey Mouse toys, dolls, books, plates, cups, cards, figurines and other items—merchandise bearing the image of Disney characters were tremendously popular sellers. Now children appeared everywhere wearing the big-eared mouse hats worn by the Mousketeers. There were Donald Duck T-shirts, Snow White bedspreads, Goofy coloring books, Peter Pan puzzles, Cinderella phonograph records, and Pluto bubble bath. There was no way of knowing what percentage of the world's population was keeping time on a Mickey Mouse watch.

Walt Disney had long ago ceased being a cartoonist and animator, and he was no longer just a filmmaker. Now he was a man of vast creative ambition who was in a category by himself. After decades of struggles, triumphs, and setbacks, Walt Disney's enterprises now brought in staggering amounts of money. Disney was elevated to a level of success unprecedented in the field of entertainment.

With TV shows, cartoons, animated features, live-action movies, an amusement park, and the various merchandising efforts, Walt Disney Productions had truly become an international entertainment empire.

9

Disney's World

The years following the opening of Disneyland marked a new phase in Walt Disney's life. His studio was involved in as many as a dozen projects at a time for theater and television, so he had little time to offer his keen insights or dabble in the production of each of them. Much of his time increasingly was spent in expanding and improving the various attractions at Disneyland. The rest of his time was spent with his growing family.

By 1957 Walt had one grandson and two granddaughters by his daughter Diane. He enjoyed them immensely, and looked forward to more when his daughter Sharon announced that she was getting married.

In 1959 Sharon married an architect named Bob Brown.[1] Sharon's marriage left Walt and Lillian Disney with an empty nest. Despite the eternal child in Disney, Sharon's marriage was an unmistakable sign of his advancing age. Walt was beginning to feel every bit of his fifty-nine years.

That same year, 1959, also saw the release of Disney's most expensive animated feature yet—*Sleeping Beauty*. It was a handsome film, full of rich detail, fine animation, and beautiful music. But the film suffered from a lack of Walt's special touch. He had only limited involvement in the story sessions, and his busy schedule had prevented him from meeting regularly with his artists to review the film's progress. Although visually impressive, the high cost of producing its rich imagery caused it to lose money on its first release.

Live-action films such as *Swiss Family Robinson* and *Pollyanna*, starring Hayley Mills, were very entertaining and did quite well at theaters. The next animated feature, *101 Dalmations*, had more warmth and character than *Sleeping Beauty*, and did much better at the box office. The popular success of *Old Yeller*, a heartrending story about a dog, led the studio to make more movies about animals.

As the studio churned out its busy schedule of movies, Walt Disney was now in his mid-sixties and growing rather tired of film work. In fact, he noticed that he was growing rather tired, period.

His collection of aches and pains were beginning to stack up. They were the result of a workaholic lifestyle in which he had allowed himself too little sleep, too many eat-and-run meals, and far too many cigarettes. His sense of his mortality was becoming quite real. He had even explored the science of cryogenics. This science deals with freezing an ailing or aging person until the time arrives when that person could be revived and restored to health.[2]

Disney could not deny that he was feeling a disturbing loss of energy and vigor. The growing realization that he may not have many years left filled him with a sense of urgency. As usual he found a creative outlet for that urgency. He wanted to produce at least one more shining achievement that would be a landmark in the history of entertainment. He believed that he had the makings of that achievement in the upcoming production of *Mary Poppins*. Disney immersed himself in its production with all his old fervor.[3]

Through Walt's guidance, *Mary Poppins* was made into something special. Just as in *Snow White and the Seven Dwarfs*, Disney was shooting for a perfect combination of story, characters, and music. The song-and-dance segments were to be very important to the vibrant energy of the film, so those chosen to play the lead characters had to be very talented singers and dancers as well as fine actors. Disney chose Broadway actress Julie Andrews to play the title role of Mary Poppins. Dick Van Dyke, a big United States television star at the time, was selected to play the role of the chimney sweep Bert.

Beautiful sequences of animation were combined with live-action to give the film some lively and truly inspired moments. The songs "Just a Spoonful of Sugar" and "Supercalifragilisticexpialidocious" were charming and inventive. They greatly added to the sense of the magical and seemingly all-wise nanny Mary Poppins.

Mary Poppins opened with an all-star gala premiere in Hollywood on August 27, 1964. Disney was decked out in a black tie and tuxedo. He was surrounded by all the Disney characters on hand to greet the arriving stars. The film was a phenomenal success, hailed by audiences and critics alike. It earned more than $44 million in its first release and was nominated for an astounding thirteen Academy Awards. The film won five Oscars—Film Editing, Original Score, Best Song, Special Visual Effects, and finally, Julie Andrews as Best Actress.[4]

The success of *Mary Poppins* prompted a whole new round of praise for Walt Disney. The long shower of honors reached its peak in September 1964. President Lyndon Johnson invited Disney to the White House to receive the Presidential Medal of Freedom, the nation's highest civilian honor. At the ceremony Johnson read the award's citation: "Artist and impressario, in the course of entertaining an age, Walt Disney has created an American folklore."[5]

While *Mary Poppins* was in production, Disney was also discussing with his Disneyland architects and designers the possibility of developing *another* Disneyland. For the new project, which they believed would eventually be sited in Florida, Walt envisioned a park quite different from Disneyland.

Disney wanted to build something that went beyond a conventional amusement park. He wanted its centerpiece to be an experimental City of Tomorrow where people really lived and worked. Disney hoped that his City of Tomorrow would be a showcase for technical innovations that would improve the quality of urban living. It would be a place that would demonstrate, by example, the ways in which progress could alter and improve people's lives.

To help experiment with ideas for possible attractions at a new park, Disney agreed to develop several attractions for the 1964 World's Fair in New York. The projects included the Carousel of Progress, for General Electric; It's a Small World, for Pepsi Cola; the Magic Skyway, for Ford Motors; and the display that most fascinated Disney, Great Moments with Mr. Lincoln, for the state of Illinois. Great Moments with Mr. Lincoln featured what was called an "Audio-Animatronic," a life-sized, electronically-controlled figure of Abraham Lincoln that was incredibly lifelike.[6]

After the 1964 World's Fair, the Disney company started to buy thousands of acres of swampland in southwest Florida near Orlando. The fact that Disney was the buyer of the land was kept a secret—lest the selling price of additional adjoining acreage would skyrocket. When it was rumored in 1965 that Disney was the buyer, the land prices leaped from $200 an acre to around $1,000 an acre, but by then the buying was nearly complete.

When the buying was finished, Disney had spent more than $5 million to purchase almost forty-three square miles of southwest Florida. The area was nearly one hundred and fifty times bigger than Disneyland.[7] Designs were already taking shape for the City of Tomorrow, which had become Disney's latest creative obsession. The city was by far the most ambitious endeavor of the proposed new park. It was to be called EPCOT, which stood for Experimental Prototype City of Tomorrow.

On New Year's Day 1966, Disney was honored as Grand Marshal of the Tournament of Roses Parade in Pasadena, California. As the year progressed he continued his plans for EPCOT and other attractions at the new park that was to be called Disney World. Another animated feature, *The Jungle Book*, was living up to the high Disney standard—as were a full slate of other live-action films.

At the same time Walt Disney's health was worsening. He was experiencing increased discomfort in his neck and lower back. Doctors told him that he would eventually need an operation to relieve the pain. Then, on November 2, 1966, X rays revealed a dark, walnut-sized mass in his left lung. Forty years of smoking had caused lung cancer in Disney.

Less than a week later, Disney underwent surgery to remove the mass. But the surgeon discovered that the cancer was in its advanced stages. Disney's entire left lung had to be removed. Unfortunately, the cancer had already spread even further. At the conclusion of the surgery, while Walt recovered, the surgeon described the operation to Lillian and her two daughters. The doctor informed them that Walt had between six months and two years to live.

In his last weeks Disney was very ill and in great pain. He tried to work and have a hand in all his various projects, but his activities were, mostly, an effort to see everyone for the last time. He returned to St. Joseph's Hospital near the studio on November 30. He received constant visits from Lillian, his daughters, his grandchildren, and of course, Roy—who had been faithfully looking out for his little brother Walt all his life.

At midnight on December 15, Walt requested the head of his bed be elevated so that he could look out the window at his studio. Roy had ordered that all the lights of the studio be kept on until further notice.[8] At 9:35 A.M., on the morning of December 15, 1966, Walt Disney died.

As Walt Disney entered his sixties, he began to show and feel his age.
In December 1966, Walt Disney died of lung cancer at the age of
sixty-five.

News of Disney's death was at first kept a secret. This allowed his family to mourn and conduct his funeral in private. Walt Disney's body was cremated and interred at Forest Lawn Cemetery in Hollywood Hills, California. Following a small private ceremony the day after his death, the news was released to the world that Walt Disney was dead.

Writers and thinkers everywhere struggled to describe what Walt Disney had meant to them and to the world. Eric Sevareid of the *CBS Evening News* said:

> He probably did more to soothe troubled human spirits than all the psychiatrists in the world. . . . what Walt Disney seemed to know was that while there is very little grown-up in a child, there is a lot of child in every grown-up. To a child this weary world is brand new; Disney tried to keep it that way for adults.

A writer for *The New York Times* commented:

> He had a genius for innovation; his production was enormous; he was able to keep sure and personal control over his increasingly far-flung enterprise; his hand was ever on the public pulse. He was, in short, a legend in his own lifetime—and so honored many times over. Yet none of this sums up Walt Disney. . . .[9]

10

The Disney Tradition

Walt Disney had left behind a legacy that was likely to last for generations. His films and cartoons were shown and reshown on television, and were periodically rereleased to the theaters. The audience response to the rerelease of his old animated classics was always positive. And the growing crowds at Disneyland showed that Walt's park and the imaginary worlds it brought to life were more popular than ever. But what about Disney World?

In October 1971, the first part of the new park in Florida was dedicated and opened to the public. Roy Disney was on hand for the dedication of the park, which he had insisted on renaming Walt Disney World.

Two months later, on December 21, 1971, Roy Disney died of a cerebral hemorrhage. The two brothers

Without the support and hard work of Walt Disney's brother Roy (pictured here with his wife in 1966) most of Walt's creative visions, from Mickey Mouse to Disneyland, would never have become realities.

from Marceline, Missouri—who had first made history by presenting Mickey Mouse to the world—were both gone.

It was now up to a new generation of Disneys and others inspired by Walt's imagination to carry on the Disney legacy. Walt's son-in-law Ron Miller and Roy's son Roy E. Disney struggled in the chaotic years after Walt's death to keep Walt Disney Productions focused on Disney-type entertainment. This was a challenge in the rapidly changing entertainment marketplace of the 1970s and early 1980s. The company trudged along with competent but only moderately successful animated features such as *The Rescuers* and *The Fox and the Hound.* But a crisis finally hit in 1984, as costs for a confused animated feature called *The Black Cauldron* mounted and Disney stock prices fell.[1]

In August 1984 Ron Miller resigned from his position on the Disney board of directors, and Roy E. Disney took control of the new board. Shortly thereafter the board of directors appointed Michael Eisner and Frank Wells to head Walt Disney Productions. Eisner then brought over Jeffrey Katzenberg from Paramount Pictures. The two newcomers immediately went to work revamping the Disney studio's entire operation.

One of their first decisions was to go ahead with production for the next animated feature *The Great Mouse Detective.* This well-done story did respectable business at theaters. Next was the elaborate live-action and animation spectacular *Who Framed Roger Rabbit*. Released in 1987, *Who Framed Roger Rabbit* was a great leap forward in animation technique and a huge success for the new Disney regime.

But the great triumph in animation that set the studio back on the inspired path Walt had set for it was *The Little Mermaid*. The wonderful story of a young mermaid who defies her father by falling in love with a human prince earned $84 million in theaters in the United States and Canada alone. Its later release on video sold eight million videocassettes.[2]

The Little Mermaid set the new standard of excellence that the studio would follow with *Beauty and the Beast, Aladdin, The Lion King, Pocahontas,* and others. Just weeks after *The Lion King* became available on videocassette, it ranked as not only the best-selling videotape ever, but the single best-selling entertainment item of all time. It appeared that the Disney tradition of artistic excellence, technical innovation, and brilliant storytelling that appealed to the child in all of us had returned and would continue.

But if this is the Disney tradition, does that mean Walt Disney was an artist, an innovator, a storyteller? He was perhaps all of these, or a combination of them.

One day in the late 1940s, a small boy approached Disney and asked him if he drew Mickey Mouse. No, Disney admitted to the boy, not anymore. Then the boy asked Walt if he thought up all the jokes and ideas in

The spirit of Walt Disney will continue to entertain, inspire, and stimulate our imaginations for generations to come.

Mickey's movies. Disney scratched his head and confessed that he no longer did that either.

"Mr. Disney, just what do you do?" the boy asked.

Walt had to think for a moment. "Well," he said, "Sometimes I think of myself as a little bee. I go from one area of the studio to another and gather pollen and sort of stimulate everybody. I guess that's the job I do."[3]

Stimulating people was a job Walt Disney loved. The vast influence of his creative genius will continue to stimulate the imaginations of people of all ages for a long time to come.

Chronology

1901—Born on December 5.

1906—Disney family moves to farm in Marceline, Missouri.

1909—Farm is auctioned after Elias Disney's bout with typhoid; family moves to Kansas City.

1910—Disney attends school in Kansas City and works
-1917   as a newspaper delivery boy.

1917—Spends summer working as a news butcher on the Pacific Railroad; moves to Chicago in fall.

1918—Drives for the Red Cross in France at the end of World War I.

1919—Works as commercial artist at Pesmen-Rubin Commercial Art Studio in Kansas City.

1920—Founds Iwerks-Disney Commercial Artists with Ub Iwerks, then takes animation job with Kansas City Film Ad Company.

1921—Begins marketing his own "Newman Laugh-O-Grams" cartoons to the Newman theater in Kansas City.

1923—Newman Laugh-O-Gram Films declares bankruptcy; Disney moves to Hollywood; brother Roy joins Walt to produce *Alice* comedies, forming Disney Brothers' Studios.

1925—Disney marries Lillian Bonds on July 13.

1927—Produces *Oswald the Lucky Rabbit* cartoons for Universal Pictures.

1928—Loses control of Oswald character to Universal; Disney creates another character—Mickey Mouse—and produces two Mickey cartoons; develops process for synchronizing sound to animation; *Steamboat Willie,* the first sound cartoon and starring Mickey Mouse, premieres in New York on November 18.

1929—Introduces *Silly Symphonies* cartoon series.

1932—Produces *Flowers and Trees,* the first color cartoon; receives special Oscar for creation of Mickey Mouse, and for *Flowers and Trees*—the first Oscar awarded to an animated cartoon.

1933—Cartoon *Three Little Pigs* is a sensation in theaters; daughter Diane is born on December 18.

1934—Work begins on *Snow White and the Seven Dwarfs.*

1937—Walt and Lillian adopt daughter Sharon; *Snow White and the Seven Dwarfs* premieres December 21; first animated feature ever is phenomenally popular and hailed as a masterpiece.

1938—Mother dies in gas furnace accident; Walt receives special Oscars for *Snow White and the Seven Dwarfs.*

1940—*Pinocchio* and *Fantasia* do disappointing business.

1941—Disney Studio workers strike; studio thereafter becomes unionized; father dies; *Dumbo* is released; studio buildings occupied by army personnel after Pearl Harbor bombing.

1942—Studio produces government information films;
-1945   *Bambi* is released; war years leave the studio financially gutted.

1946—Disney begins producing live-action and nature
-1948   films to recover studio's financial footing.

1949—Disneys buy new home; indulges in a large model train and many other hobbies, brainstorming about an amusement park.

1950—*Cinderella* animated feature is biggest Disney success since *Snow White*; *Treasure Island,* Disney's first big live-action hit is released.

1951—*Alice in Wonderland* and *Peter Pan* are released
-1953   to theaters; plans commence for an amusement park.

1954—Daughter Diane marries; *Disneyland* television show premieres.

1955—Disneyland amusement park opens on July 17; *Mickey Mouse Club* show appears on television in October.

1959—Daughter Sharon marries; Disney notices health slipping; *Sleeping Beauty* is released.

1964—*Mary Poppins,* Disney's last great innovative film achievement, premieres in Hollywood on August 27.

1964—Land is bought in Orlando, Florida, area for
-1965   Disney World park.

1966—Diagnosed with lung cancer in November; Walt Disney dies in hospital near his studio on December 15.

Chapter Notes

Chapter 1

1. Bob Thomas, *Walt Disney: An American Original* (New York: Hyperion, 1994), p. 275.

Chapter 2

1. Leonard Mosley, *Disney's World* (Lanham, Md.: Scarborough House, 1990), p. 24.

2. Bob Thomas, *Walt Disney: An American Original* (New York: Hyperion, 1994), p. 24.

3. Katherine and Richard Greene, *The Man Behind the Magic: The Story of Walt Disney* (New York: Viking/Penguin, 1991), p. 8.

4. Mosley, p. 30.

5. Barbara Ford, *Walt Disney* (New York: Walker & Company, 1989), p. 13.

6. Thomas, pp. 40–41.

7. Mosley, p. 38.

8. Ibid., p. 39.

Chapter 3

1. Marc Eliot, *Walt Disney: Hollywood's Dark Prince* (New York: Carol Publishing Group, 1993), pp. 12–13.

2. Bob Thomas, *Walt Disney: An American Original* (New York: Hyperion, 1994), p. 45.

3. Eliot, pp., 12–13.

4. Thomas, p. 54.

5. Ibid., p. 55.

6. Katherine and Richard Greene, *The Man Behind the Magic: The Story of Walt Disney* (New York: Viking/Penguin, 1991), p. 35.

7. Bob Thomas, *Disney's Art of Animation* (New York: Hyperion, 1991), p. 34.

Chapter 4

1. Bob Thomas, *Walt Disney: An American Original* (New York: Hyperion, 1994), p. 70.

2. Leonard Mosley, *Disney's World* (Lanham, Md.: Scarborough House, 1990), pp. 76–77.

3. Ibid., p. 80.

4. Katherine and Richard Greene, *The Man Behind the Magic: The Story of Walt Disney* (New York: Viking/Penguin, 1991), p. 45.

5. Ibid., p. 48.

6. Bob Thomas, *Disney's Art of Animation* (New York: Hyperion, 1991), p. 75.

7. Marc Eliot, *Walt Disney: Hollywood's Dark Prince* (New York: Carol Publishing Group, 1993), pp. 34–35.

8. Ibid.

Chapter 5

1. Bob Thomas, *Walt Disney: An American Original* (New York: Hyperion, 1994), pp. 88–90.

2. Leonard Mosley, *Disney's World* (Lanham, Md.: Scarborough House, 1990), p. 108.

3. Ibid.

4. Thomas, p. 95.

5. Ibid., p. 96.

6. Katherine and Richard Greene, *The Man Behind the Magic: The Story of Walt Disney* (New York: Viking/Penguin, 1991), pp. 59–60.

7. Ibid., p. 60.

8. Mosley, p. 129.

Chapter 6

1. Marc Eliot, *Walt Disney: Hollywood's Dark Prince* (New York: Carol Publishing Group, 1993), pp. 55–56.

2. Ibid., p. 58.

3. Leonard Mosley, *Disney's World* (Lanham, Md.: Scarborough House, 1990), pp. 132–133.

4. Ibid., p. 133.

5. Ibid., p. 132.

6. Bob Thomas, *Walt Disney: An American Original* (New York: Hyperion, 1994), p. 114.

7. Bob Thomas, *Disney's Art of Animation* (New York: Hyperion, 1991), p. 19.

8. Ibid., p. 49.

9. Mosley, p. 150.

10. Ibid.

11. Thomas, *Art of Animation*, p. 65.

12. Leonard Maltin, *The Disney Films* (New York: Crown Publishers, 1973), p. 12.

13. Ibid., p. 28.

14. Thomas, *Art of Animation*, p. 77.

15. Eliot, p. 102.

Chapter 7

1. Katherine and Richard Greene, *The Man Behind the Magic: The Story of Walt Disney* (New York: Viking/Penguin, 1991), p. 77.

2. Ibid., p. 78.

3. Leonard Mosley, *Disney's World* (Lanham, Md.: Scarborough House, 1990), pp. 189–191.

4. Ibid., p. 195.

5. Ibid., p. 208.

6. Bob Thomas, *Disney's Art of Animation* (New York: Hyperion, 1991), p. 91.

7. Bob Thomas, *Walt Disney: An American Original* (New York: Hyperion, 1994), p. 179.

8. Greene, pp. 110–113.

Chapter 8

1. Bob Thomas, *Walt Disney: An American Original* (New York: Hyperion, 1994), p. 241.

2. Ibid., pp. 249–250.

3. Ibid., pp. 264–270.

4. Ibid., p. 275.

5. Leonard Mosley, *Disney's World* (Lanham, Md.: Scarborough House, 1990), pp. 248–249.

Chapter 9

1. Katherine and Richard Greene, *The Man Behind the Magic: The Story of Walt Disney* (New York: Viking/Penguin, 1991), p. 137.

2. Marc Eliot, *Walt Disney: Hollywood's Dark Prince* (New York: Carol Publishing Group, 1993), pp. 140–143.

3. Ibid.

4. Leonard Maltin, *The Disney Films* (New York: Crown Publishers, 1973), p. 232.

5. Bob Thomas, *Walt Disney: An American Original* (New York: Hyperion, 1994), p. 328.

6. Greene, p. 156.

7. Ibid., p. 157.

8. Eliot, p. 256.

9. Thomas, p. 354.

Chapter 10

1. Bob Thomas, *Disney's Art of Animation* (New York: Hyperion, 1991), p. 112–114.

2. Ibid., p. 120.

3. Bob Thomas, *Walt Disney: An American Original* (New York: Hyperion, 1994), p. 222.

Further Reading

Fanning, Jim. *Walt Disney*. New York: Chelsea House, 1994.

Ford, Barbara. *Walt Disney: A Biography*. New York: Walker & Company, 1989.

Greene, Katherine, and Richard Greene. *The Man Behind the Magic: The Story of Walt Disney*. New York: Viking Penguin, 1991.

Mosley, Leonard. *Disney's World*. Lanham, Md.: Scarborough House, 1990.

Thomas, Bob. *Disney's Art of Animation*. New York: Hyperion, 1991.

———. *Walt Disney: An American Original*. New York: Hyperion, 1994.

Index

92
Dis

Cole, Michael D.

Walt Disney.

$18.95   26450

DATE			

BAKER & TAYLOR